Tropical Rain Forests

PETER BENOIT

Children's Press®
An Imprint of Scholastic Inc.
New York   Toronto   London   Auckland   Sydney
Mexico City   New Delhi   Hong Kong
Danbury, Connecticut

Content Consultant
Molly Cavaleri, PhD
Michigan Technological University
Houghton, Michigan

Library of Congress Cataloging-in-Publication Data

Benoit, Peter, 1955–
  Tropical rain forests/Peter Benoit.
     p. cm. — (A true book)
  Includes bibliographical references and index.
ISBN-13: 978-0-531-20554-9 (lib. bdg.)   978-0-531-28103-1 (pbk.)
ISBN-10: 0-531-20554-1 (lib. bdg.)   0-531-28103-5 (pbk.)
  1. Rain forest ecology—Juvenile literature. 2. Rain forests—Juvenile literature. I. Title.
  QH541.5.R27B44 2011
     577.34—dc22   2010045935

All rights reserved. Published in 2011 by Children's Press, an imprint of Scholastic Inc.
Printed in China. 62
SCHOLASTIC, CHILDREN'S PRESS, A TRUE BOOK and associated logos are trademarks and/or registered trademarks of Scholastic Inc.

8 9 10 11 12 R 18 17 16 15 14

Find the Truth!

Everything you are about to read is true **except** for one of the sentences on this page.

Which one is **TRUE**?

T or F   Less than half of all living insect species are known by scientists.

T or F   Most tropical rain forest plants live on the forest floor.

Find the answers in this book.

3

Contents

THE **BIG** TRUTH!

The Race to the Top

**White-fronted
capuchin monkey**

← Rain forest termites can help break down dead tree parts in a matter of weeks.

**Poisonous
tree frog**

This man looks tiny compared to the towering trees of the Costa Rican rain forest.

6

CHAPTER 1

The Rain and Heat

Imagine walking into a tropical rain forest. You feel a carpet of leaves beneath your shoes. The smell of wet soil fills your nostrils. The air is hot, wet, and noisy. Before long, you are sweating. Birds, insects, monkeys, and other animals are chirping and chattering. Far below the treetops, the forest floor is dark. The space is full of trees, vines, and mist.

The tallest trees in rain forests can grow up to 292 feet (89 meters)!

A Long, Long Time Ago

Tropical rain forests covered most of the land 100 million years ago. Earth was warmer and wetter than it is today. Sixty million years later, the planet's **climate** began to cool off. It became drier. Tropical rain forests began to shrink. The areas left behind became deserts and grasslands. Cooler forests developed in many parts, where trees lost their leaves in the colder months.

Grasslands today often flourish near the edges of tropical rain forests.

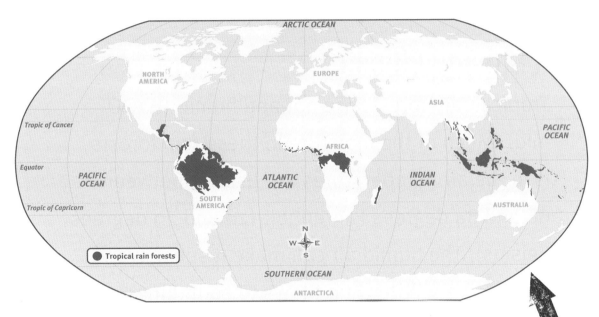

This map shows Earth's tropical rain forests.

More than half of the world's tropical rain forests are found along the Amazon River.

Tropical rain forests lie on the **equator**. This area is home to the hottest places on Earth. Where the climate is wet enough, tropical rain forests bloom. The largest are in central Africa and along the Amazon River in South America. They are also found in Central America, Australia, Asia, and several islands in the Pacific.

A Steamy Climate

Tropical rain forests are hot and humid (HYOO-mid). Much of the moisture in these rain forests is in the air. Temperatures are usually between 68 and 84 degrees Fahrenheit (20 and 29 degrees Celsius). The humid air can make it seem even warmer. Very little wind blows to cool things off.

Rain forest air is so moist that clouds of mist often float overhead.

Cloud cover keeps temperatures from rising too high.

Heavy rainfall is one reason so many plant species grow in rain forest ecosystems.

Most tropical rain forests have no dry season. They get rain all year, with about 100 inches (250 centimeters) falling each year.

Temperature and rainfall change very little throughout the year. In fact, the temperature changes more between day and night than it does between summer and winter.

The layers of a rain forest are visible in this illustration.

CHAPTER 2

Layer Upon Layer

Tropical rain forests are like living, leafy cakes. How? They're set up in layers, one on top of the other, a bit like the layers of a cake. Each layer is a little different from the ones above and below. Different plants and animals can be found in each layer. The amount of moisture and light changes, too.

 In nature, the layers sometimes blend into each other and can be difficult to tell apart.

The Emergent Layer

The highest layers are the emergent (ee-MUR-jint) layer and the **canopy**. The emergent layer is the very tops of the trees. This is where the sun shines and raindrops first land. The forest's tallest trees are usually 150 to 180 feet (45 to 55 meters) high. Strong winds blow against the treetops. These tall trees must be strong to withstand the winds. Bats, butterflies, and some monkeys live in this layer.

Capuchin monkeys live in the canopy but may visit the lower levels to play.

About half of all plant species grow in tropical rain forest canopies.

The forest canopy is packed tightly with the leaves and branches of tall trees.

The Canopy

Closely packed treetops form an unbroken cover of leaves and branches. This canopy is dense. It stands about 130 feet (40 m) above the ground.

Living among the treetops are millions of plants. Flowering plants such as orchids (OR-kidz) grow up here. So do mosses, fungi (FUHN-jye), and algae (AL-gee). Orchids attach to trees with their clinging roots. Many animals in the emergent layer above also live in the canopy.

The Understory and Shrub Layers

Below the canopy are the understory and shrub layers. These are much darker than the layers above. Only about 5 percent of the available sunlight makes it through the canopy. The herbs, ferns, vines, and small trees growing here live with very little sunlight.

Countless birds and reptiles live here. So do boa constrictors, which can grow up to 14 feet (4 m) long. Jaguars and leopards can also be found in some rain forests.

Emerald tree boas spend much of their time coiled around branches in South American rain forests. They rarely visit the forest floor.

Termites live and travel together in large groups.

A single colony of rain forest termites can have millions of insects.

The Forest Floor

The forest floor receives only about 1 percent of the forest's sunlight. Very few plants live here. Instead, the ground is covered mostly by dead leaves and other matter. Termites and even smaller living things eat away at it, so that it **decomposes** into nutrients that plants can use for food.

Parrots are known for their colorful feathers and ability to learn words.

CHAPTER 3

A Crowded Space

Tropical rain forests are crowded with life. They contain more than half of all plants and animals living on Earth. This is more than any other ecosystem. All of these living things have **adapted** to the moist heat of rain forests. Most can climb or fly to reach places high in the trees. Some never touch the ground.

Parrots are found in every tropical rain forest in the world.

Can you spot the stick insect hiding among the rain forest plants?

 Scientists believe the majority of insects have yet to be discovered.

Crawlers and Climbers

Insects are the most **diverse** (dye-VURSS) living things in the tropical rain forest. There are possibly millions of different species. Ants and termites live everywhere, from the highest parts of the canopy all the way down to the ground. Stick insects, which look just like their name, crawl among the twigs and branches of the trees. There are also flying insects, including beetles, bees, moths, and butterflies.

Colorful Wildlife

The tropical rain forest includes millions of other animals. Like insects, most of them can fly or climb. Birds and bats are common flyers. Several kinds of monkeys climb through the rain forests. They have long arms to reach between branches.

Many animals are brightly colored. Birds-of-paradise use their colors to attract mates. Small, poisonous tree frogs use their coloring as a warning to animals that might try to eat them.

Some frogs have solid-colored skin, while others have interesting patterns.

Among the Trees

Millions of tropical rain forest plants are known. Still, new ones are found every year.

About 70 percent of rain forest plants are trees. Many other plants depend directly on trees for survival. Most, such as orchids or moss, do not harm the tree. A plant called the monster flower does harm trees. It steals moisture and nutrients from the tree. Its huge, red flower blossoms on the tree's roots, attracting flies with its awful smell.

The monster flower can grow as large as 3 feet (1 m) across.

The weight of several orchids has been known to topple trees.

There are more than 22,000 species of orchids.

A Leg Up

Orchids have adapted to the rain forest in an interesting way. They attach themselves to trees, high above the forest floor. Here, they reach the sunlight, but their roots never touch the ground. Instead, rain washes over them, bringing with it fallen plant material, which the orchids use for food. The tree is not harmed by this process.

So Many Different Trees

Trees are perhaps the most important part of the tropical rain forest. They are extremely diverse. Even within a small area, several different kinds of trees can easily be found.

Most rain forest trees are evergreen. They hold on to their leaves all year round. Some drop their leaves when it gets too dry. Leaves at the top of the canopy are usually small and thick. Leaves near the bottom are bigger and thinner. This helps them soak up more light.

24

The average rain forest tree lives between 100 and 500 years.

The Xingu people live in Brazil's Amazon rain forest.

People of the Forest

Many people live near the edges of tropical rain forests. They use rain forest land and **resources**, but their communities are located outside of the forests.

Thousands more live in tribes inside the world's rain forests. Most have very little contact with people outside the forest. Some, such as the pygmies (PIHG-meez) in Africa, mostly hunt and gather. The Yanomami (yah-noh-MAH-mee) and Kayapo (kah-YAH-poh) of the Amazon do some farming.

The Race to the Top

Sunlight is an important resource anywhere. In tropical rain forests, it is also very limited. As little as 4 hours of sunlight reaches the forest through the clouds. Most of this light never makes it far beyond the treetops. New trees must wait for older trees to fall or die. When they do, a space is left, allowing sunlight through. New trees rush to fill in the space to survive.

Some plants and trees grow very quickly and fill in much of the gap. Others continue to grow slowly under their shade.

When a gap opens, the sun reaches the young trees. It also warms the soil on top of the waiting seeds. Growth speeds up.

Young trees grow very slowly underneath the canopy. Some seeds simply lie and wait for the chance to grow.

The seeds of some rain forest trees have wings that slow their fall.

Here, a child picks fruit from an annatto tree. The seeds are used in a variety of products, including food and makeup.

28

CHAPTER 4

The Rain Forest's Many Uses

Tropical rain forests have a lot to offer us. Many of the things we use every day come from them. They give us food and lifesaving medicine. The wood of certain rain forest trees is a valuable building material for homes and businesses. Tropical rain forests also play a large part in keeping Earth livable. Everyone in the world uses the rain forest for something.

 Annatto fruits are also called *urucum*, which means "red" in Tupi, a local language.

Using the Plants

The tropical rain forest can save a life. As much as one-fourth of the world's natural medicines come from tropical rain forests. Scientists believe that thousands more have not even been discovered yet. The plants found there can keep a heart healthy or cure an illness. There are even plants that can help a headache!

Scientists continue to develop new medicines from rain forest plants.

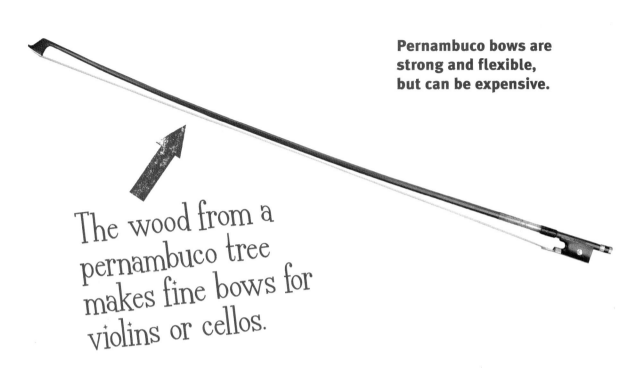

Pernambuco bows are strong and flexible, but can be expensive.

The wood from a pernambuco tree makes fine bows for violins or cellos.

The Source of Food and Shelter

Wood is another valuable resource. This can be used for anything from firewood to building a house. Furniture, such as chairs and desks, is often made using wood from the rain forest.

The trees can also provide fruit, such as mangos, bananas, and pineapples. Some trees produce **latex**. This can be used to make rubber tires or latex gloves.

Farmers create rich farmland by burning tropical rain forests.

Using the Land

Trees are sometimes cleared so the land can be used for farming. Farmers usually use a **slash and burn** method. First, trees and smaller plants are cut down, or slashed. Then the farmer sets fire to the slashed plants. The ash from the plants leaves the soil healthier, making it easier to grow crops. Common crops are sugar, cocoa, and soybeans.

Raising Animals

Tropical rain forest land is also cleared to raise cattle. Cattle graze on large areas of land. These cows are then sold as meat. Most of this meat is sent to other countries.

A rain forest's water is also important. It provides drinking water to people living in or near the forest. Rivers can provide power. The energy of a river's flow can be used to produce electricity.

Cattle ranching is the biggest source of forest loss in the Amazon.

Scientists continue to learn more about rain forests by studying the rich diversity of plant and animal life found there.

Living and Learning

Tourists often visit tropical rain forests. People come to see the plants and animals that exist only in the rain forest. Scientists come to study. Many hope to find new medicines. Others search for undiscovered species.

Tropical rain forests are also a home. Countless animals and plants live there. About 240 million people live in or near them.

Warm, but Not Too Warm

Carbon dioxide (dye-OX-ide) is a gas. Humans and animals produce it when they breathe. It is also produced in massive amounts by cars and factories. This gas helps trap the sun's heat, warming the planet. If there is too much carbon dioxide, too much heat is trapped. This harms the planet.

Tropical rain forests are a **carbon sink**. Trees absorb carbon dioxide from the air. It is stored in their roots, trunks, and branches. Rain forests help keep the planet in balance.

Rush hour traffic in Toronto, Ontario, Canada

Huge portions of the Amazon rain forest are being cut to make room for farmland.

CHAPTER 5

Delicate Balance

People have lived around rain forests for thousands of years. For most of that time, tropical rain forests have thrived. People used forest resources without damaging the environment. Lately, this balance has been lost. Tropical rain forests are quickly shrinking. People around the world are looking for ways to stop this. What happens as we lose the rain forest?

 Rain forests are being destroyed faster than any other ecosystem.

Losing Too Many Trees

People clear land to grow crops and raise cattle. They also cut down trees to sell as lumber. This is called **deforestation**. Too much farming or grazing can lead to overuse of the land. These activities take necessary minerals from the soil. The forest is unable to grow back. Plants, animals, and people lose their homes. Some species go **extinct**.

Timeline of Tropical Rain Forests

100 million years ago
Tropical rain forests cover most of Earth's land.

65 million years ago
An asteroid hits Earth, changing its climate. Two-thirds of the planet's species disappear.

38

Gone Forever

When a species becomes extinct, there are no more of that species left. Some species go extinct because they lose their home. Animals need space to live. Sometimes there is no longer enough food to go around. This can also cause a species to die out. Scientists believe that between 100 and 1,000 species out of every million become extinct each year.

40 million years ago
The climate cools and dries. Tropical rain forests shrink.

1900
Tropical rain forests cover about 12 to 15 percent of Earth's land.

2011
Tropical rain forests cover about 6 percent of Earth's land.

An increase in carbon dioxide around the planet can change weather patterns.

Climate Change

When land is cleared, it loses its trees and other plants. Plants are no longer there to trap carbon. Carbon sinks are lost. This means that more carbon is being released. This carbon joins the gases that are already keeping our planet warm. This layer of gases becomes thicker and thicker. The planet becomes warmer and warmer. This leads to global warming, or **climate change**.

The Ever-Changing Earth

Some climate change is natural. Earth's weather patterns change regularly over millions of years. A dry, cold Earth changes to a wet, warm one and back again. Rain forests have naturally grown and shrunk.

Many scientists today, however, believe people are causing climate change to happen too quickly. The planet is becoming too warm, too fast. Life on Earth cannot keep up.

Global temperatures may rise as much as 7°F (4°C) by the year 2100.

Factory production is one of the many human activities that is adding to climate change.

Finding a Solution

Thousands of people work to save tropical rain forests. Some plant trees. Others tell the public about what is going on. They might create Web sites or hand out flyers. Still others work with governments. They hope to create new laws that help protect the forests.

We all need to do our part and work together to protect our tropical rain forests. ★

Planting new trees is just one of the many ways people can work to help save Earth's rain forests.

True Statistics

Amount of Earth's land covered by tropical rain forests: 6 percent

Portion of Earth's plants and animals living in tropical rain forests: More than half

Average rainfall: 100 in. (250 cm)

Average temperature: 68°F to 84°F (20°C to 29°C)

Largest tropical rain forest: The Amazon in South America

Size of largest tropical rain forest: 2.1 million sq. mi. (5.4 million sq km)

Country with largest portion of tropical rain forests: Brazil, with more than 30 percent

Amount of tropical rain forest lost each year: About 54,000 sq. mi. (140,000 sq km)

Number of species that become extinct each year: Between 100 and 1,000 out of every million

Did you find the truth?

T Less than half of all living insect species are known by scientists.

F Most tropical rain forest plants live on the forest floor.

Resources

Books

Kenyon, Linda. *Rainforest Bird Rescue: Changing the Future for Endangered Wildlife*. Buffalo, NY: Firefly Books, 2006.

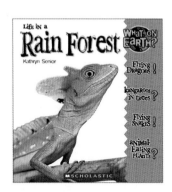

Mason, Paul. *Forests Under Threat*. Chicago: Heinemann Library, 2009.

McKenzie, Precious. *Rainforests*. Vero Beach, FL: Rourke Publishing, 2011.

Moore, Heidi. *Rain Forest Food Chains*. Chicago: Heinemann Library, 2011.

Sen, Benita. *Rainforest Creatures*. New York: PowerKids Press, 2008.

Senior, Kathryn. *Life in a Rain Forest*. New York: Children's Press, 2005.

Simon, Seymour. *Tropical Rainforests*. New York: HarperCollins Publishers, 2010.

Sobol, Richard. *Breakfast in the Rainforest: A Visit with Mountain Gorillas*. Cambridge, MA: Candlewick Press, 2008.

Welsbacher, Anne. *Protecting Earth's Rain Forests*. Minneapolis: Lerner Publications, 2009.

Organizations and Web Sites

National Geographic Kids—Tropical Rain Forests

http://kids.nationalgeographic.com/kids/photos/tropical-rainforests/

Look here for photos and interesting information about rain forests.

National Geographic—Rain Forest at Night

www.nationalgeographic.com/features/oo/earthpulse/rainforest/index_flash.html

Explore a rain forest after dark, from canopy to forest floor.

Scholastic—Pop-Up Picture

http://teacher.scholastic.com/scholasticnews/indepth/rainforest/popups.asp

Learn about everyday items that come from rain forest materials.

Places to Visit

American Museum of Natural History: Hall of Biodiversity

Central Park West at 79th Street
New York, NY 10024-5192
(212) 769-5100
www.amnh.org/exhibitions/permanent/biodiversity/
Don't miss a stunning rain forest exhibit.

Smithsonian National Zoological Park: Amazonia Exhibit

3001 Connecticut Ave. NW
Washington, DC 20008
(202) 633-4480
nationalzoo.si.edu/Animals/Amazonia/Exhibit/default.cfm
Tour an enclosed tropical habitat at the National Zoo's largest exhibit.

Important Words

adapted (uh-DAPT-id)—changed to suit a certain purpose or situation

canopy (KAN-uh-pee)—dense cover of leaves and branches

carbon sink (KAR-buhn SINGK)—a location where carbon is absorbed

climate (KLYE-mit)—the normal or average weather of an area

climate change (KLYE-mit CHAYNJ)—change in Earth's usual weather patterns

decomposes (dee-kuhm-POH-zuz)—rots, decays, is eaten away

deforestation (dee-for-eh-STAY-shuhn)—the clearing of a forest area of plant life

diverse (dye-VURSS)—having variety

equator (i-KWAY-tur)—an imaginary line running around Earth, halfway between the North and South Poles

extinct (ek-STINGKT)—died out

latex (LAY-teks)—a milky liquid used to make rubber

resources (REE-sorss-iz)—things that are valuable or useful

slash and burn (SLASH AND BURN)—a method of farming in which plants are cut down and then burned

Index

Page numbers in **bold** indicate illustrations

About the Author

Peter Benoit is educated as a mathematician but has many other interests. He has taught and tutored high school and college students for many years, mostly in math and science. He also runs summer workshops for writers and students of literature. Mr. Benoit has also written more than 2,000 poems. His life has been one committed to learning. He lives in Greenwich, New York.